# Speaking Skills

## L. Ann Masters, Administrator

Curriculum and Instructional Program Improvement Unit
Nebraska Department of Education
Lincoln, Nebraska

### Merle Wood

Education Consultant
Formerly of Oakland Public Schools
Lafayette, California

## South-Western Publishing Co.

Developmental Editor: Mark Linton
Production Editor: Karen Roberts
Associate Director/Design: Darren Wright
Production Artist: Sophia Renieris
Associate Photo Editor/Stylist: Kimberly A. Larson
Associate Director/Photography: Diana W. Fleming
Assistant Photographer: Mimi Ostendorf
Marketing Manager: Shelly Battenfield

**Cover: Stamp design © 1991 United States Postal Service**

ISBN: 0-538-70778-X

1 2 3 4 5 6 7 8 9 0 DH 98 97 96 95 94 93 92
Printed in the United States of America


For permission to reproduce the photograph on the page indicated, acknowledgment is made to the following:

*UNIT 1*     p. 9: Best Western International, Inc.

# PREFACE

SPEAKING SKILLS presents basic information for the improvement of speaking skills. This text-workbook is written specifically for the adult learner and is designed to permit self-paced, individualized instruction and foster student success.

The main focus of SPEAKING SKILLS is improving the student's speaking skills. The student will realize through this text-workbook that speaking is a valuable communication skill and good speaking skills in the workplace are essential for job success. Students will also learn how to prepare and deliver a presentation.

## SPECIAL FEATURES

SPEAKING SKILLS is designed specifically to help you invest in the future of your adult learners and to meet your instructional needs. Some features of the text-workbook include the following:

• A larger typeface is used to make the text-workbook easier for students to use and to read. Pages are colorful and uncrowded.

• Content and examples relate to adult-level, real-life issues and skills.

• Pretests and posttests with answers and evaluation charts are included for self-evaluation.

• Competency-based methodology is used. Clear objectives and short segments of instruction are followed by student activities for immediate reinforcement.

• Study breaks provide refreshing and useful information that contributes to the general literacy of the student.

• Abundant exercises are included, each designed so that students experience frequent and meaningful success.

• Goals are listed for each exercise to provide motivation and direction.

• All exercises are supported with Bonus Exercises for students who need a second chance to succeed.

• Answers to all exercises are included to facilitate independent, self-paced learning.

• Personal progress is recorded by the student after completing each exercise.

• Individual success is measured by evaluation guides in the student's Personal Progress Record.

## INSTRUCTOR'S MANUAL

The Instructor's Manual provides instructional strategies and specific teaching suggestions for SPEAKING SKILLS along with supplementary bonus exercises and answers, additional testing materials, and a certificate of completion.

**Bonus Exercises.** A bonus exercise, matching each exercise in the text-workbook, is provided in the manual. These bonus exercises make it possible for students to have a second chance to reach the goals set for each exercise. Answers to the bonus exercises are also provided in the manual. These materials may be reproduced for classroom use.

**Testing Materials.** Two additional tests along with answers are provided in the manual to allow for more flexible instruction and evaluation.

**Certification of Completion.** Upon completion of SPEAKING SKILLS, a student's success may be recognized through a certificate of completion. This certificate lists the skills and topics covered in this text-workbook. A certificate master is included in the manual.

# CONTENTS

Everyone who is capable of speaking uses the skill every day. You will speak in many situations—talk with friends, give directions to strangers, provide information for co-workers, and perhaps even have an occasion to accept the challange of speaking to a group.

SPEAKING SKILLS will assist you with the task of improving the way you present yourself and your ideas as you speak. The text-workbook will also help you evaluate and improve your present speaking voice.

## HOW YOU WILL LEARN

SPEAKING SKILLS is written with you in mind. You will learn the skill of expressing yourself in many situations on the job and in your personal life. There is a system used in this book that will help you learn.

### Learn at Your Own Pace

You will progress through the lessons in this book at your own pace. If you move ahead faster, or go slower, than other students, don't be concerned. You are to work at *your* best speed.

### Learn Skills Successfully

You will be given objectives and goals for each unit. You will know what you are to accomplish. You will study a topic, then you will complete an exercise. This will let you practice what you have just learned. When you have shown that you know the topic, you will move on to the next topic. You will always know just how well you are doing as you move through each step in this book.

### Complete Bonus Activities

You may not reach your goal on every practice exercise. When this happens, you should review the lesson and then complete a Bonus Exercise. These exercises cover the same lessons as the practice exercises in this book. They give you a second chance to reach your goal. When you score higher on a Bonus Exercise than you did on the original activity, you may change your score on your Personal Progress Record. Your instructor has copies of these Bonus Exercises and the answers to them.

## Check Your Own Success

You will keep track of your own success and check all of your own work. The answers are in the back of this book. The color-tinted pages make them easy to find. Always do the exercises before you look at the answers. Use the answers as a tool to verify your work—not as a means of filling in the blanks. You will record your scores on your own Personal Progress Record, which is also in the back of this book.

## WHAT YOU WILL LEARN

As you study SPEAKING SKILLS, you will learn how to use your speaking skills more effectively. Your ability to speak is important to your ability to communicate correctly.

In Unit 1, Speaking and Communicating with Others, you will learn about the role speaking plays in your ability to communicate your thoughts to others.

In Unit 2, Speaking in the Workplace, you will learn more about the settings in which you will be speaking on the job. You will learn more about the role of speaking in a job interview, how to communicate with your co-workers, and how to ask questions.

In Unit 3, Polishing Your Speaking Skills, you will learn how to improve the sound, quality, and clarity of your voice so that others will be better able to understand the messages you are sending.

In Unit 4, Your Chance to Speak Out, you will learn the fundamentals of how to prepare and deliver a speech before others. You will learn that speaking to a group is not the terrifying task you may envision.

## SPECIAL FEATURES

SPEAKING SKILLS has a number of special features. These features will help you learn and apply the material successfully.

## Checking What You Know

You can check what you already know about speaking before you start studying this book. Checking What You Know identifies those skills you need to improve upon. Then, when you complete this book, you will do an exercise called Checking What You Learned. By comparing these two scores, you will see how much you have gained through your study.

## Putting It Together

Each unit has a number of short exercises called Checkpoints. These exercises will help you check your understanding of a specific topic before continuing. At the end of each unit you will find a section titled, "Putting It Together". This section contains several exercises that are similar to the Checkpoints. They will help you to reinforce the skills you learned in each unit.

## Personal Progress Record

You will keep track of your own progress. Once you check your answers, you will record your score on your Personal Progress Record at the end of this book. After you finish a unit, you will be able to see your level of success.

## Certificate of Completion

When you finish your study in this book, you may be eligible for a certificate of completion. Your instructor will explain to you the skill level required for this award.

## READY TO START

You are now ready to start improving your ability to use your speaking skills. Through your study and completion of the exercises, you should quickly develop an improved ability to communicate through speaking.

Your improved skill will prove to be of benefit to you. You can do both your personal and on-the-job speaking with added confidence. You should also have improved opportunities to move up the job ladder where, in many cases, well-developed speaking communication skills are required.

Turn to page ix and complete Checking What You Know. Check your answers on page 59. Then begin Unit 1, Speaking and Communicating with Others.

# CHECKING WHAT YOU KNOW

Take this pretest before starting SPEAKING SKILLS. The 25 questions will tell you how much you already know about speaking. They will also tell you what you need to learn.

There is no time limit, so don't rush. When you finish, check your answers. Give yourself 2 points for each correct answer. Record your score on your Personal Progress Record. After finishing this book, you will be able to see how much you learned.

DIRECTIONS:   Read each of the following statements. If the statement is true, write a T in the space provided. If it is false, write an F in the space provided.

_____ 1. Listening to the sound of a bird is communicating.
_____ 2. The only purpose of messages is to give information or direction.
_____ 3. A message sent without words is a verbal message.
_____ 4. The actions of the receiver of a message are called communicators.
_____ 5. The circle of communication is complete when the sender's message reaches the receiver.
_____ 6. A loud booming voice is needed in the workplace.
_____ 7. A major part of speaking on the job will be sharing and providing information to others.
_____ 8. Avoid referring questions to others.
_____ 9. Persuasion is an attempt to get others to disagree with you.
_____ 10. Avoid asking questions in a job interview.
_____ 11. What you say at the employment interview may determine whether or not you get the job.
_____ 12. Your vocal cords vibrate to create the vocal sounds.
_____ 13. Each person's voice is different.
_____ 14. Your brain, nervous system, vocal cords, and throat work to make you speak.
_____ 15. Pitch is the loudness or softness of your voice.
_____ 16. A monotone voice has good expression.
_____ 17. Good posture commands respect.
_____ 18. Your facial features may say more than your words.
_____ 19. The purpose of the introduction of a speech is to tell the audience what you want them to know.
_____ 20. Practicing a speech will make the speech sound unnatural.
_____ 21. Avoid meaningless and repeated gestures when you are giving a speech.
_____ 22. Apologize to the audience if you get stuck for a word or thought while speaking.
_____ 23. The best way to conclude a speech is to tell a joke.

_____ 24.   In developing a speech, consider the interests and needs of the audience first.

_____ 25.   Lean against the podium or a wall for support as you present a speech.

☞ *Check your work on page 59. Record your score on page 63.*

# UNIT 1

## Speaking and Communicating with Others

## COMMUNICATING

You probably enjoy some of these speaking and listening situations everyday—listening to the radio, talking with a friend or neighbor, listening to the sound of a bird, or giving directions to a stranger. All of these activities are called *communicating*.

### What Is Communication?

*Communication is the process of sending and receiving information.*

The process of sending and receiving information is called **communication**. You are continually involved in communication. If you ask a friend to help lift a heavy box and the friend helps you, you are communicating. If your neighbor asks you for a ride, and you say "sure," you are communicating.

### What Is a Message?

*A message is the item of communication being sent or received.*

The item of communication that you are sending or receiving is known as the **message**. Communication transfers a thought or idea from the sender to the receiver. Life would be boring and perhaps impossible without communication.

## RECEIVER OR LISTENER

Part of communicating is what you hear. When you hear, you are receiving information. Therefore, you are called a *receiver* or *listener*. A listener or receiver accepts information.

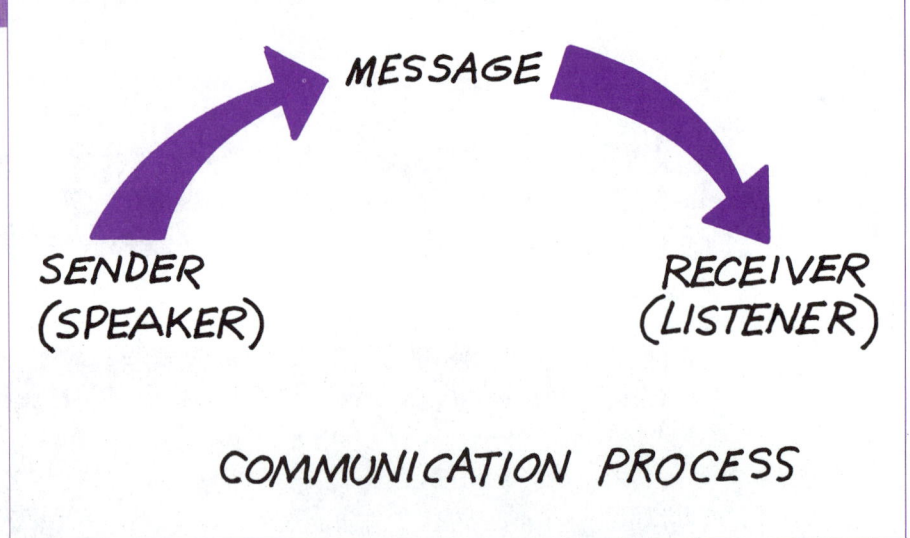

Illustration 1-1

Communication process.

## What Do You Hear?

Each day of your life you listen or receive information. You listen to the radio or a television set. You listen to the noises of the city—the sounds of cars, the voices of people passing you on the street, the blare of a radio from a cruising car, the whistle of a police officer, or the scream of a siren from a fire truck. Or maybe you listen to the sounds of the country life—the whistle of the wind, the babble of a stream, the whinny of a horse, the song of a bird, or the voice of a bullfrog. Whatever your life style, you do a lot of listening.

## What Do You Receive?

As you listen to others, and the sounds of the city or country, you are actually hearing or receiving. What you hear are the messages of communication. The messages give you information or direction, warn you of danger, alert you to the needs of others, or relax your mind. You may be able to think of other messages or sounds you hear within a day.

## MESSAGES FROM OTHERS

That which we are capable of feeling, we are capable of saying.

—Cervantes

Speak, that I may see thee.
          —Ben Jonson

Only the educated are free.
          —Epictetus

## CHECKPOINT 1–1

**YOUR GOAL:**
Get 4 answers correct.

In the space provided, list two messages or sounds most often heard in the city. You will get 1 point for each blank completed.

1. _____

2. _____

In the space provided, list two messages or sounds you received from someone today. You will get 1 point for each blank completed.

1. _____

2. _____

In the space provided, list two messages or sounds you like to receive in the country. You will get 1 point for each blank completed.

1. _____

2. _____

☞ *Check your work on page 59. Record your score on page 64.*

## SENDER OR SPEAKER

In your daily routine, you are not always the listener or receiver of a message. Many times, you have the opportunity to be the sender or speaker of a message. When you are in the role of the sender, you send a thought or idea to someone else. When that idea or thought is spoken or sent to someone else, you are a sender or speaker of a message.

### What Do You Send?

As the speaker, you may send information. For example: "The grocery store is on Adams Street." "Your shoe is untied." "The bus stops here at 9:15 a.m." You may provide others with directions. You may attempt to talk others into agreeing with you. Sometimes you speak to praise or thank others. For example: "Thanks for your help." "Bob, your work on my house was great." As the speaker or sender, you may protect someone by providing a warning. "Watch out for that beam!" "The dog bites." "The bus is turning."

Illustration 1-2

Providing information—one duty of the sender.

## CHECKPOINT 1–2

**YOUR GOAL:**
Get 8 answers correct.

In the space provided, list four messages which give information that you have sent or may send today. You will receive 1 point for each information message.

1. _____

2. _____

3. _____

4. _____

In the space provided, list four warnings you have given today or in the past. You will receive one point for each warning.

1. _____

2. _____

3. _____

4. _____

In the space provided, write two directions you have given or plan to give today. You will receive one point for each direction.

1. _____

2. _____

☞ **Check your work on page 59. Record your score on page 64.**

## How Do You Send?

As a speaker or sender, you usually send messages with your voice. The sound of your voice helps others understand what you say. A firm, loud voice helps the receiver of your message know you are serious. A soft, gentle voice tells your receiver you are sending a kind message.

## KINDS OF MESSAGES

Messages are sent in many ways. The words "good morning" spoken to another indicate that you want someone to have a pleasant morning. You nod your head to send the message that someone was noticed. You point at the clock and indicate that time is important.

## Verbal Messages

A verbal message is a message sent with words.

When you say "good morning," "hi," or "goodbye," you use your voice. In many ways your voice is you. You are the only person who has just that voice. Your friends do not have to see you to recognize you. All they have to do is hear your voice. When you use your voice to send a message, this is called a **verbal message.** An example of a verbal message might be: "Shut the door." "I hope you are feeling better." "I enjoyed the movie."

## Nonverbal Messages

A nonverbal message is a message sent without words.

You may choose to send a message by an action. No spoken words are required. A message sent without using words is a **nonverbal message.**

You may wave to someone entering your work area. This physical action signals to your co-worker that you are saying "hello." No words were necessary. A neighbor may look at you and roll his or her eyes. This action sent you a message. What was it? Keep in mind the old saying, "Actions speak louder than words." If your words give one message and your nonverbal message gives another, the nonverbal message is stronger.

## CHECKPOINT 1–3

**YOUR GOAL:**
Get 3 answers correct.

In the left column are five common actions. In the space provided in the right column, write the message you would receive from the nonverbal message. You will receive 1 point for each nonverbal message described.

1. The tapping of a pencil.                    _____

2. A tight fist raised above the head.         _____

3. The tapping of a foot.                      _____

4. Crossing the arms on the chest.             _____

5. Pointing a finger.                          _____

☞ **Check your work on page 59. Record your score on page 64.**

Share your answers with others. Are your answers the same? There may be some differences. Nonverbal messages can easily be misunderstood.

## CHECK MESSAGES

How can you be sure that the message you send is correctly received? How do you know if your co-worker thinks the joke you told is funny? How can you tell if your boss believes your excuse for being a few minutes late? How do you know if your friend likes your new shoes? How do you know if your sister shares your feeling that the temperature is too warm?

### Watch the Listener

In order to check your message, you should watch the actions of the receiver. The actions of the receiver usually tell you how accurately the message has been received. If you tell a co-worker a joke and the reaction is laughter, you can assume the co-worker "got the joke" and thought it was funny.

## MESSAGES FROM OTHERS

When in doubt, tell the truth.
                    —Mark Twain

No man pleases by silence; many please by speaking briefly.
                                        —Ausonius

Illustration 1-3

Keep your eye on the receiver.

## What Are the Actions Called?

The actions of the receiver of a message are called **feedback**. You arrive at work five minutes late and tell your boss you were caught in traffic. The boss responds with a quick up and down nod and walks off. The feedback indicates that your explanation was accepted. You ask a friend, "How do you like my new shoes?" The feedback is "They look great," and the friend nods his or her head. You know your friend understood the question and likes your shoes. Remember, feedback may come in the form of a verbal or nonverbal message.

Feedback is the listener's response that tells the sender if the message is understood.

After feedback is added to the communication process, it looks like Illustration 1-4. The sender sends a message. The message is "Get on the bus." The receiver receives the message, nods, and gets on the bus. The sender knows the message is complete because of the actions of the receiver.

*Feedback is the listener's response that tells the sender if the message is understood.*

## THE CIRCLE OF COMMUNICATION

The circle of communication is not complete when the sender's message reaches the receiver. The circle is only complete when the receiver's feedback reaches the sender to end the process. Illustration 1-4 shows you how good communication is a two-way process.

If you tell Fido, "Sit!" and Fido doesn't sit, the circle of communication is not complete between you and Fido. Fido did not receive the message. You will need to try again.

**Illustration 1-4**

Circle of communication.

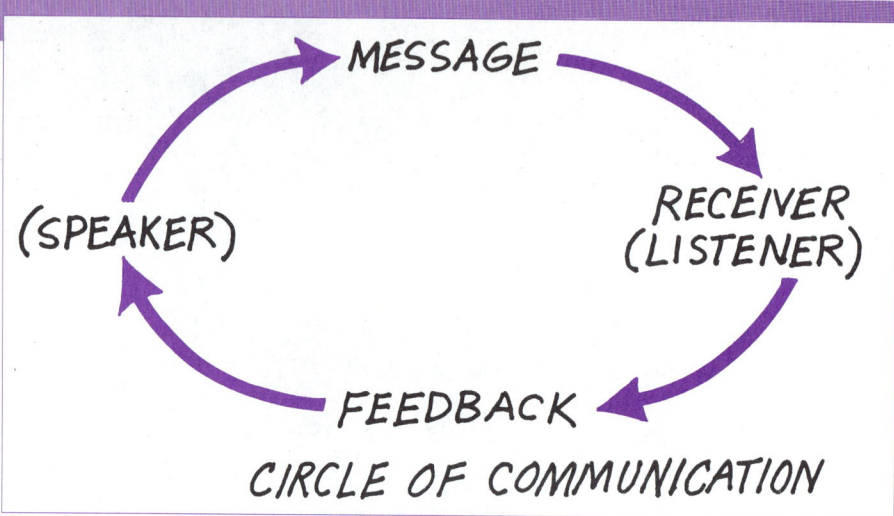

### Senses that Help Complete the Circle

*The channel is the route that a message takes to get to the receiver.*

People use their senses as well as words to complete the circle of communication. The senses can help the two-way process. The route that a message takes to get to the receiver is called the **channel**. Sound waves are the channel related to the sense of hearing when verbal messages are sent. The sense of sight is involved with the channel through which visual (sight) messages are sent. If the sense of touch is used, the channel is the skin.

If Fido doesn't sit after the sound-wave message is sent, you may want to try again using another channel. Try the touch channel this time. Place your hand on Fido's rump and push down. If Fido sits, you know the circle of communication is complete.

### Additional Senses

Many times you will use more than one of your senses to help get a message across. For example, you say to a person, "I'm sorry you are feeling ill." You have used the verbal channel to send your message. To add additional meaning to your message, you squeeze the hand of the person. You have added the touch channel. The receiver of the message squeezes your hand, and you know the message was communicated.

## CHECKPOINT 1–4

**YOUR GOAL:**
Get all 3 answers correct.

Place an X in the space provided for the channel of communication which will be used to complete the communication process in these examples. Give yourself 1 point for each correct answer.

|  | **Sight** | **Sound** | **Touch** |
|---|---|---|---|
| ● A teacher determines that Arthur wants to answer a question. | X | | |
| 1. Business people greet each other with a handshake. | | | |
| 2. Dad feels the head of a child after the child complains of a headache. | | | |
| 3. Two friends talk on the phone. | | | |

☞ **Check your work on page 59. Record your score on page 64.**

## WHAT YOU HAVE LEARNED

- The process of sending and receiving information is called communication.
- Receiving or listening is receiving and/or accepting information.
- Sending or speaking is sending a thought or idea to someone.
- Messages sent to others may be sent with words (verbal messages) or actions (nonverbal messages).
- Checking to see if your message has been received is done by observing the receiver.
- The actions of the receiver are feedback.
- The circle of communication is complete when the message has gone from the sender to the receiver and back to the sender.

## ACTIVITY 1-1 YOUR GOAL: Get 3 answers correct.

Locate a cartoon in a local newspaper which shows an example of the circle of communication. Attach the cartoon to this page. Answer the question about your cartoon in the spaces provided. Give yourself 1 point for each correct anwer.

1. What is the message the sender wanted the listener to receive?

   _____

2. Was the message received correctly by the listener?

   _____

3. What additional words or nonverbal actions would have helped the speaker send the message?

   _____

4. What additional channels could the speaker have used to get the message across?

   _____

5. What signs of feedback do you see in the cartoon?

   _____

☞ **Check your work on page 59. Record your score on page 64.**

## ACTIVITY 1-2 YOUR GOAL: Get 5 answers correct.

In the space provided, list five nonverbal actions that you see in a single day. Watch for those actions on television and as you talk with and watch others. Give yourself 1 point for each correct answer.

● **Scratching the head** _____

1. _____

2. _____

3. _____

4. _____

5. _____

☞ **Check your work on page 59. Record your score on page 64.**

## ACTIVITY 1-3 YOUR GOAL: Get 3 answers correct.

What message(s) would you receive in the following settings? No verbal messages are given in addition to what you are seeing. Write your answers in the spaces provided. Give yourself 1 point for each correct answer.

- A woman dressed in a beaded, long gown.

  **The woman is going to a party. The woman is rich.**

1. A man wearing a ski jacket has his leg in a cast.

   _____

   _____

2. A shivering woman on a park bench with a paper sack beside her.

   _____

   _____

3. A student slumped down on a desk.

   _____

   _____

4. A picture of the Statue of Liberty with fireworks in the background.

   _____

   _____

5. A woman with tears in her eyes walking out of a hospital.

   _____

   _____

☞ *Check your work on page 60. Record your score on page 64.*

# UNIT 2

## Speaking in the Workplace

### WHAT YOU WILL LEARN

When you finish this unit, you will be able to:
- Prepare mentally to be a speaker in the workplace.
- Understand the situations that will require you to be a speaker in the workplace.
- Speak appropriately in special situations in the workplace.

## PREPARATION FOR BEING A SPEAKER

You will be a speaker in the workplace. You will be a better speaker and communicator if you are prepared mentally.

### How Do You See Yourself?

Take a look in the mirror. What do you see? You should see a person who has ideas and thoughts to share. You must recognize the value of your thoughts and ideas in order to communicate them. How many times have you been close to sharing an idea and then backed away? Then, a few moments later, someone else has the same idea, shares it, and is recognized for it. Now is the time for you to see yourself in your own mind as a worthy person. You are a worthy person with ideas and thoughts to express in the workplace.

### How Do You Feel?

As you think about speaking and sharing with others, it is natural to feel a little uneasy. The best speakers, actors, and communicators get a few butterflies before speaking. The thought of speaking with others in the workplace should not be frightening. You were hired because you are a qualified worker. You were hired to share and communicate with others. Think positively of yourself, and others will think positive thoughts of you. Remember, you were chosen for the position.

Others can hear anger, sadness, happiness, and other emotions in your voice. In some cases, you may want to wait until you have control of your emotions. Remember to breathe to

**Illustration 2-1**

How do you
see yourself?

keep oxygen going to your brain. You can think better when
you breathe. You gain control of your emotions when you
breathe.

## How Do You Sound?

Listen to the sound of your voice. You may have a very soft
voice. Perhaps your voice is difficult to hear. You will want to
speak up. Make an extra effort to be sure that others hear
what you have to say.

You may have a booming voice. Your voice may be too loud
and bother others within the work area. You will need to work
at toning down your voice. Speak more softly, but be sure to
speak clearly.

You will want to appear skillful, competent, and interesting as you speak on the job. You can do this by feeling good
about yourself and following the points in Illustration 2-2.

**Illustration 2-2**

Points to
remember
when speaking
on the job.

### POINTS TO REMEMBER WHEN SPEAKING ON THE JOB

1. Don't try to impress others.
2. Be yourself.
3. Use your own words as you ask questions or
   provide input.
4. Think about what you are saying.
5. Control your emotions—breathe.
6. Speak clearly and not to softly or loudly.

## CHECKPOINT 2-1

**YOUR GOAL:**
Get 3 or more answers correct.

In the space provided, complete the following statements about the points to remember when speaking on the job. The first one is completed as an example. Give yourself 1 point for each correct answer.

● Don't try to __impress__ others.

1. _____ yourself.

2. Use your own words as you ask questions or _____ input.

3. Think about what you are _____ .

4. _____ your emotions—breathe.

5. Speak _____ and not too softly or too loudly.

☞ **Check your work on page 60. Record your score on page 64.**

## SPEAKING SITUATIONS ON THE JOB

You developed your speaking skills as you grew from childhood. You will also develop speaking skills in communicating with others as you grow on the job. You will be asked to share information and ideas, contact others, help solve problems, and influence others while you are on the job. Each speaking situation requires a review of Illustration 2-2.

### Sharing and Providing Information

A major part of your speaking on the job will be sharing with and providing information to others. The basic rules for sharing information with co-workers, customers, and supervisors are the same. Let's take a look at the rules:

1. *Be polite.* Show an interest in providing the information that is being requested. Your words and the tone of your voice must be polite. Be eager and willing to share information.

   RAMON:   Jason, can I ask you a question?
   JASON:   Sure, I'll try to help.

2. *Be sure that you understand what is being asked.* Restate the information you think is being requested. Use your own words to rephrase the question.

> RAMON:  Jason, will you tell me how to find the paper we use for covers on the booklets sent to the Wong Corporation?
>
> JASON:  Sure, I think I can help. You want to know how to find the paper we use for covers on booklets we produce for the Wong Corporation.
>
> RAMON:  That's right.

3. *Share what you know.* Be specific in providing information. Provide all the information you know. If printed information, a sketch, or some type of drawing would be helpful in sharing information, *use it.*

> JASON:  Look in the file drawer labeled paper stock. Pull the file marked "Wong Corporation." You will find the stock number of the paper used on booklets for Wong. Susie, the stockroom clerk, will find the paper for you if you provide her with the number.
>
> RAMON:  Thanks for your help.

4. *Refer to another person if you don't know.* If you don't know or are not sure of the information being asked, try to help by referring the person to someone else. You may need to assist her or him in finding others who can provide the information needed.

5. *Ask if the information you have shared is adequate.* To complete the circle of communication, be sure to check your feedback with the person you are providing information for.

> JASON:  Does that take care of what you needed to know?
>
> RAMON:  Sure does. Thanks again.

6. *Don't use the sharing of information as an opportunity to start or continue a nonwork-related conversation.* You should provide the information requested in a willing manner and go on with your work.

> JASON:  By the way, do you know of any sales on bowling balls? I sure would like to pick up a new ball before the fall season starts.

7. *Show that you are willing to provide help and share information in the future.* Your willingness to help will encourage others to continue to ask for help. You will build goodwill with co-workers, customers, and supervisors.

> JASON:  Always glad to help. Let me know if you find the paper.

## MESSAGES FROM OTHERS

Confidence does more to make conversation than wit.

—La Rochefoucauld

A good conversationalist is not one who remembers what was said, but says what someone wants to remember.

—John Mason Brown

## CHECKPOINT 2–2

**YOUR GOAL:**
Get 6 or more answers correct.

Place a T in the space provided if the statement is true. Place an F in the space provided if the statement is false. The first one is completed as an example. Give yourself 1 point for each correct answer.

___**F**___ • Do not refer questions to another person.

_____ 1. Do not use an illustration to answer a question.

_____ 2. Politeness in answering questions is important.

_____ 3. Restate a question if you are not sure what was asked.

_____ 4. Use your own words when you rephrase questions.

_____ 5. A major part of speaking on the job will be sharing information with others.

_____ 6. Use the sharing of information as a way to start a nonwork-related conversation.

_____ 7. Avoid referring questions to others.

_____ 8. Check to make sure the information shared is adequate.

☞ **Check your work on page 60. Record your score on page 64.**

## Requesting Information

You will often need to seek information from others. You will need to ask questions of your co-workers, supervisors, and perhaps even customers. Before you ask a co-worker or a supervisor for information, be sure that you have tried to find the answer first. You don't want to take up the time of others unless it is necessary.

You may need to request information from customers in order to better understand their needs. For example:

| | |
|---|---|
| YOU: | Marshall's Hardware. May I help you? |
| CUSTOMER: | Yes, I would like some burner covers for my range. |
| YOU: | What brand of range do you own? |
| CUSTOMER: | I have a Top-Point. |
| YOU: | Is your Top-Point fueled by gas or electricity? |
| CUSTOMER: | It is a gas range. |
| YOU: | Do you have a particular color in mind? The covers come in harvest gold, almond, and black. |

Your questions should help the customer clarify his or her order. These questions will help the customers get what they want.

## Requesting Action

Sometimes you may need to ask a co-worker to do something for you. State your questions or requests for action so that they are easily understood. State your requests in simple terms. Most people like straightforward questions. A good way to state your request is using the AEA request formula explained in Illustration 2-3.

Illustration 2-3

Request formula.

### HOW TO MAKE A ROUTINE REQUEST

**A** = Ask for the information or action to be taken.

**E** = Explain your need in brief terms.

**A** = Appreciate by thanking your supervisor or co-worker for the help and cooperation.

For example, see how Vincente asks Carol to trade lunch hours, provides a brief explanation, and then expresses appreciation.

| | |
|---|---|
| VINCENTE: | Carol, I would like to trade lunch hours with you on Thursday. I need to go to lunch from 12:30 to 1:30 p.m. My scheduled hour is 11:30 a.m. to 12:30 p.m. I want to see my son in a school program. Are you willing to trade with me? |

The feedback from your request will let you know if the request was understood.

CAROL:      Vincente, I will be glad to trade lunch hours with you on Thursday. Please remind me on Wednesday of our agreement.

VINCENTE:   Thanks. I appreciate your willingness to help me. I'll talk with you on Wednesday.

## Persuading Others

**Persuasuion** is attempting to get others to adopt or agree with an idea that you have. On-the-job speaking will include getting others to agree with you.

Persuasion is attempting to get others to adopt or agree with an idea that you have.

You will want and need at various times to persuade customers, co-workers, and supervisors. Part of your job may be to persuade customers to use a product or service of your employer.

You will need to get the attention of the customer, co-worker, or supervisor. You must show your audience why your idea, product, or service is the best. Two ways to persuade others are discussed. One approach is to ask a question:

Did you know one glass of our juice provides 90 percent of the vitamins your baby needs?
Would you like to help the people of your community?

The questions are positive and bring to mind happy thoughts. These questions put your listener in the mood to hear what you have to say. The question approach is very good for persuading customers.

LOU:   Oki, do you want what is best for your baby?

OKI.   Of course!

JOHN:  Would you like to save money on gas?

JUDY:  Sure, how can I do that?

Another approach is to tell a story. Everyone likes to hear a good story. The story must relate closely to the message you want your customer, co-worker, or supervisor to hear. Keep your story brief. The story doesn't have to be funny. The story probably will be about something you have experienced in your life. An example of a story to persuade follows:

Let me tell you about my friend Elmer. Elmer thought he didn't need to join in the fun of a block party. He chose to just sit on his porch and watch. One of the kids threw him a ball. Of course, he wanted to throw it back. Before Elmer knew it, he was joining in the fun. I know

## ◀ MESSAGES FROM OTHERS

Watch your speech. A person's command of the language is more important. Next to kissing, it's the most exciting form of communication mankind has evolved.

—Oren Arnold

you would enjoy bowling with us after work. Do you want to give it a try?

Perhaps a story like this one would help you to get a co-worker to join the department bowling team. Other stories could help get a supervisor to listen to an idea of yours or persuade a customer to try a new product or service.

## ✔ CHECKPOINT 2–3

**YOUR GOAL:**
Get 3 or more answers correct.

Complete the following statements with the words at the end of the statements. Write the words in the space provided. The first one is completed as an example. Give yourself 1 point for each correct answer.

- Before you ask a co-worker or supervisor for information, be sure you have tried to find the answer **first**.

1. Your _____ can help the customer clarify his or her order.

2. State your _____ so that they are easily understood.

3. The AEA formula means ask, _____, and appreciate.

4. Persuasion is the _____ to get others to agree with you.

5. To persuade a customer, you may ask a question or tell the customer a_____ .

Attempt, Explain, First, Questions, Requests, Story.

☞ **Check your work on page 60. Record your score on page 64.**

## SPECIAL OPPORTUNITIES FOR SPEAKING ON THE JOB

You will speak in many situations on the job. You begin a job by speaking at a job interview. You will respond to questions.

You will respond to comments made by your supervisor when your work is reviewed or evaluated.

## Employment Interview

What you say at the employment interview may determine whether or not you get the job. You should prepare for the interview by thinking about some of the questions you may be asked. Be prepared to talk about your previous jobs. You will talk about your background and experiences that are related to the type of job you are applying for. Some questions you can expect might include:

"What type of work have you been doing?"

"Do you enjoy working outdoors or indoors?"

"Will you tell me a little bit about yourself?"

"Why do you feel you are qualified for this position?"

Your voice should be clear and loud enough for the interviewer to hear your answers. Look at the interviewer as you answer questions, as shown in Illustration 2-4. If you do not understand a question, ask that the question be repeated or restated. For example:

INTERVIEWER:  Have you ever worked in low coal?

AUDREY:  I don't know what you mean by low coal.

Illustration 2-4

The job interview.

Your answers should be honest and straightforward. It is all right to take a few seconds to put your thoughts together before answering a question. Avoid answering with only "yes" or "no." Try to state at least one complete thought as you respond to a question. For example: "Have you ever worked in a forestry operation?" If your answer is "no," you might say: "I haven't had the opportunity to work in forestry, but I enjoy the outdoors." If your answer is "yes," give a little information. For example: "Yes, I worked in the forests of Wisconsin as a firefighter."

## CHECKPOINT 2–4

**YOUR GOAL:**
Get 3 or more questions answered.

Write your answers to the job interview questions in the space provided. The job you are applying for is a position as a trainee with the forestry service. Give yourself 1 point for each answer you can provide.

● Why did you leave your last job?

   **My job was cut because of a slowdown in demand for the**

   **products we were building.**

1. What jobs have you held in the last two years?

   _____

   _____

   _____

2. Do you enjoy working outdoors?

   _____

   _____

   _____

3. When could you begin working?

   _____

   _____

   _____

4. Why do you think you would be successful in this position?

   _____

_____

_____

5. Are you willing to travel?

_____

_____

_____

☞ **Check your work on page 60. Record your score on page 64.**

You will want to have questions ready for the interviewer. Plan ahead. Write your questions on a small piece of paper or a card and take it with you. Some sample questions might be:

"What hours would I be working?"

"Is there a fringe-benefit package?"

"Will you tell me a little more about the job than is described in the ad?"

"Is this a permanent position?"

You will be expected to ask questions. Good questions will help the interviewer know that you are interested in the job.

## Work Reviews

Your work will be reviewed or evaluated by a supervisor. In most positions, work reviews occur at least before the end of a 90-day trial period. Your work may be reviewed again after the first six months and annually thereafter. This review should let you know how you are doing on the job. Do not look at this review as a scary or threatening situation. Look at the review as an opportunity to improve on the job. Be prepared for the review by thinking about questions you have about your work. You may want to write these questions down and take them to the review with you. You should look at the reviewer and show interest in what is being discussed. Let the reviewer know that you are listening, by responding with a nod of the head or a brief comment. For example:

REVIEWER:  Megan, I am pleased with the work you are doing as a production worker.

MEGAN:  Thank you. I enjoy my work.

The review that goes well for you is easy to respond to. You listen, you ask your questions, and then you thank the reviewer for his or her time and suggestions. However, if the review does not go well for you and you receive many suggestions--or even a warning that you will be fired--you will need to follow a different procedure. The steps in Illustration 5-5 will help you know what to do if the review is not going well for you.

Illustration 2-5

How to handle a difficult work review.

## HOW TO HANDLE A DIFFICULT WORK REVIEW

**Step 1:** Listen carefully. Give nonverbal responses to the reviewer to indicate that you are listening.

**Step 2:** Ask questions to clarify the concerns of the reviewer.

**Step 3:** If there are some differences of opinion or points of confusion about your work, state your side of the story in honest, straight-forward terms. (Be careful to keep an even tone of voice.)

**Step 4:** Indicate that you will work to improve. Ask for help in the future.

**Step 5:** Thank the reviewer for his or her time.

## CHECKPOINT 2–5

**YOUR GOAL:**
Get 3 or more answers correct.

Unscramble the letters to show the steps of handling a difficult work review. Write your answers in the space provided. Give yourself 1 point for each correct answer.

● ksA rof pleh ni eth retufu.

   **Ask for help in the future.**

1. netsiL yllfuacre.


2. skA ionstques ot yfiralc teh ccsnreno.



3. tateS ouyr edis fo teh yrots.

4. etacidnL ttah uoy llwi krow ot evorpmi.

_____

_____

5. nkahT het eewriver ofr sih ro reh emit.

_____

_____

☞ **Check your work on page 60. Record your score on page 64.**

## WHAT YOU WILL LEARN

● The importance of preparing mentally to speak in the work-place, and points to remember when speaking on the job.
● Your role in sharing and providing information, requesting information, requesting action, and persuading others.
● Tips on speaking in a job interview and in a work review.

## ACTIVITY 2–1  YOUR GOAL: Get 3 or more answers correct.

Place an X in the space provided if the response to the situation is appropriate. Place an O in the space provided if the response is not appropriate. Then briefly explain why you placed an X or an O. Give yourself 1 point for each correct answer.

- Situation: Nicolas has asked you a question about working overtime. You do not know the answer.

  <u>   X   </u> I'm sorry, Nicolas. I don't know the answer. I am sure that Elsie in the Personnel Department can help you.

  Why? <u>Answer was direct. Nicolas was directed to another person for help.</u>

1. Situation: Meredith has been working about 10 minutes trying to get a paper jam out of the copy machine. She asks for your help.

   <u>        </u> Sure. I'll try to help you. Let's get out the manual and see if paper jams are explained.

   Why? _____

   _____

2. Situation: Ileana is trying to deliver a package for her employer. The street signs are confusing. She asks for your help.

   <u>        </u> The street you are looking for is on the other side of the railroad tracks. Go to the tracks and turn left at the first traffic light. Go south about seven or eight blocks. You will see the street sign on the east side of the road.

   Why? _____

   _____

3. Situation: Tyron says to you, "Will you please show me how to get this forklift out of gear?"

   <u>        </u> Sure. All you need to do is hold down the lever marked with a red G. Can you help Joe and me move this weekend?

   Why? _____

   _____

☞ *Check your work on page 60. Record your score on page 64.*

## ACTIVITY 2–2 YOUR GOAL: Get 2 or more answers correct.

In the space provided, write what you would say to a customer or co-worker to try and persuade him or her to use the product or to agree with you. The first one is completed as an example. Give yourself 1 point for each correct answer.

- You are selling soft drinks in the stands at a major league football game.

  **Did you know that Joe Montana drinks one of these at halftime?**

1. You are trying to get a customer to sample the ice cream you are selling.

   _____

   _____

   _____

2. You want Hedy, your co-worker, to trade hours work with you, and she doesn't particularly want to.

   _____

   _____

   _____

3. You want a co-worker to try to use an easy method of bundling papers for recycling. The co-worker doesn't like change.

   _____

   _____

   _____

4. A customer prefers to use a brand of soap he or she has been using for years. You want to convince him or her that Slide Soap is better.

   _____

   _____

   _____

☞ *Check your work on page 60. Record your score on page 64.*

**ACTIVITY 2–3** YOUR GOAL: Get 2 or more answers correct.

In the space provided, write a question that you would expect at a job interview. Then write in the space provided the answer that you would give to the question. Give yourself 1 point for each correct answer.

1. Question: _____

   _____

2. Answer: _____

   _____

In the space provided, write a question you would expect to ask at a job review session.

3. _____

   _____

   _____

   _____

☞ *Check your work on page 60. Record your score on page 64.*

# UNIT 3

## Polishing Your Speaking Skills

## WHAT YOU WILL LEARN

When you finish this unit, you will be able to:

- Understand the body parts that enable you to speak.
- Improve your speaking voice by recognizing the importance of the qualities of pitch, volume, tone, and inflection.
- Recognize the importance of correct articulation and pronunciation of words used.
- Add quality to a spoken message by using correct posture, personal appearance, facial expression, and gestures.

## WHAT IT TAKES TO SPEAK

Think of speaking as a product. Speaking is a product you market every day. You have the equipment and the know-how to use it. Speaking is the way you communicate and send messages to others. The ability to speak requires that four of your body parts function together. These are the brain, the nervous system, the vocal cords, and the mouth.

### Brain

Your brain acts as a computer. The brain scans your available knowledge and sends messages to the nerves to set the muscles into action.

### Nervous System

The nervous system activates the muscles so that air is forced up from the lungs. Tiny vocal cords begin moving in the voice box in your throat.

### Vocal Cords

Your vocal cords actually vibrate to create the vocal sounds. These sounds are enlarged as they move through your throat, nose, and mouth, and create a voice that is yours alone.

## MESSAGES FROM OTHERS

The mind is a wonderful thing—it starts working the minute you're born and never stops—until you get up to speak.

—Anonymous

It takes two to speak the truth . . . one to speak and the other to hear.

—Henry David Thoreau

### Mouth

Your mouth shapes the voice into the individual sounds of your speech. Your mouth and tongue move together to shape the words correctly.

These four parts of your body work automatically together to enable you to deliver information to others. Therefore, you can spend your efforts in delivering the best sounding voice possible.

## CHECKPOINT 3–1

**YOUR GOAL:**
Get 3 or more answers correct.

Place a T in the space provided if the statement is true. Place an F in the space provided if the statement is false. The first one has been completed as an example. Give yourself 1 point for each correct answer.

**F**

_____ • Your nose shapes the voice into the individual sounds of your speech.

_____ 1. Your body parts work automatically to enable you to speak.

_____ 2. Your vocal cords vibrate to create sounds.

_____ 3. Your brain does not play a part in your ability to speak.

_____ 4. The nervous system activates your muscles so that air is forced into the lungs to allow your vocal cords to produce sounds.

_____ 5. Each voice is different.

☞ **Check your work on page 61. Record your score on page 64.**

## IMPROVING YOUR SPEAKING VOICE

There is no one right way to speak. Life would be dull if everyone spoke and sounded alike. However, there are certain characteristics of good voice and speech which you should try to apply.

In your effort to deliver a good, clear sounding voice you will need to work to control the pitch, the volume, the tone, the inflection of your voice, and other special voice qualities.

**Pitch** is the highness or lowness of a voice. The pitch is actually determined by the length, thickness, and tension of your vocal cords. You have no control over the length or thickness of your vocal cords. However, you do have control of the tension. When your vocal cords are too tense, they produce high, squeaky tones. Work at speaking easily and without strain, and your pitch will be pleasant. Ask others, "Is my voice too high or shrill? Is it too low?"

**Volume** is the loudness or softness of a sound. Others will tire quickly of a voice that is too weak and too soft to hear. Have you ever been watching television or listening to the radio that has the volume very low? If you have had this experience, you know what a strain it is to try to hear.

Listening to a very loud voice can also be very annoying. Adjust your voice so that others can hear you clearly without straining. If you are unsure of your volume, ask the help of others. Say, "Am I speaking loudly enough?" or "Am I speaking too loudly?"

Pitch is the highness or lowness of a voice.

Volume is the loudness or softness of a sound.

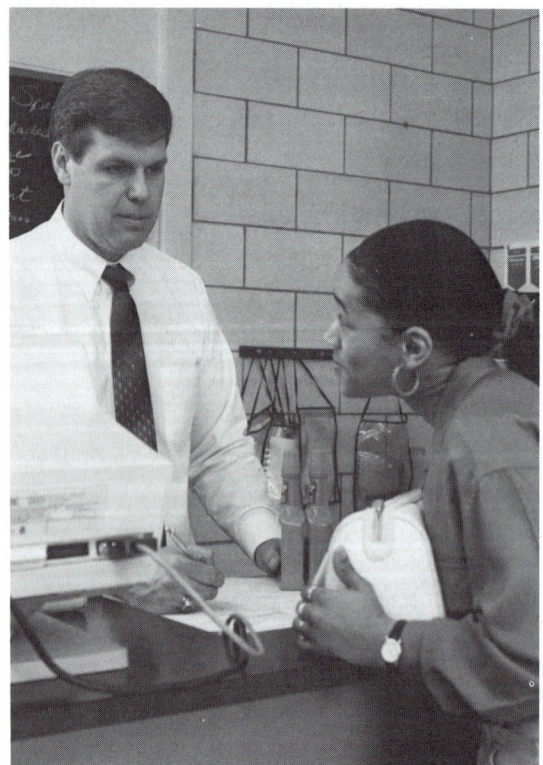 

Illustration 3-1

Check your volume.

## Tone

Tone is the quality of harshness or smoothness of a sound.

**Tone** is the quality of harshness or smoothness of a sound. The tone of your voice is the way your voice sounds. There are three sounds in English which should be produced through your nose: *m*, *n*, and *ng*. No other sounds should be produced through the nose. Say this sentence, which has no nasal sounds: "She is outside." Now pinch your nose together and say the sentence again. If you feel no pressure of air through the nose, your tone is probably good. All breath should come through the mouth. If you are unsure of your tone, ask others: "Is my voice clear and pleasing? Do I sound like I am talking through my nose?"

## Inflection

Inflection is the rising and falling of your voice.

Monotone is a voice with no expression. It always sounds the same.

**Inflection** is the rising and falling of your voice. A person who has no inflection speaks in a **monotone**. Your voice should help to express the meaning of words and sentences. Be sure your voice is not always the same. You can do this by changing your pitch, the speed at which you speak, and the volume of your voice according to your meaning. Again, check with others by asking: "Is my voice flat? Does my voice always sound the same?"

## CHECKPOINT 3–2

**YOUR GOAL:** Underline 4 or more subjects correctly.

Read the following groups of sentences aloud. Make your voice express the feelings suggested at the left. Read each line to someone else to check your progress. Give yourself 1 point for each group read effectively.

| Feelings | Sentences |
|---|---|
| Interested | 1. Are they real diamonds, Ms. Smith? |
| | 2. Eiko, did you have a good trip? |
| | 3. Did she really win the contest? |
| Pleasure | 1. Sure, I'll help you. |
| | 2. What a beautiful fall day this is! |
| | 3. Oh, thanks for your help. |
| Excitement | 1. We can go home now, Micaela! |
| | 2. The game is over! We won! |
| | 3. Frank got the tickets! |
| Worried | 1. That puppy may not have an owner. |
| | 2. We haven't seen him for a week. |
| | 3. Morris has been ill. |

☞ **Check your work on page 61. Record your score on page 64.**

## SPECIAL VOICE QUALITIES

In addition to pitch, volume, tone, and inflection, there are other qualities which make your voice easier to understand. These special qualities are articulation and pronunciation.

### Articulation

*To articulate is to make speech sounds more clearly.*

You may become lazy in forming speech sounds. To **articulate** is to make speech sounds more clearly, also called *enunciation*. The main organ of articulation is the tongue. The more carefully you articulate, the more likely you are to be understood. When you articulate or enunciate clearly, you are saying all the letters in every word. Be careful to speak each word clearly and not run words together. For example, avoid the sloppiness of running phrases together like "Havyeetnyet?" Say, "Have you eaten yet?" Also, take care not to leave parts of words unspoken. Say, "breakfast," not "brefast." With a little effort, you can make all of your words clear. In normal rapid speech, *to* may be pronounced *tuh*, and *them* may be pronounced *em*. Say "take them," not "take 'em." Say "had to," not "had tuh."

Be sure to say the *t* and *d* in phrases like "don't you." If you do not, you may end by slurring and saying *choo*, and come out with "donchoo." You should also avoid omitting the *d* or *t* altogether, as in "don'you" or "foun'you," for "don't you" and "found you." If you do not articulate these sounds, your speech is difficult to understand.

## ✔ CHECKPOINT 3–3

**YOUR GOAL:**
Read 3 groups to someone clearly.

Complete the following exercise with a neighbor, friend, instructor, or family member. Read each group to someone else. Let the other person help you decide how well you are articulating. Give yourself 1 point for each group read clearly.

1. Read aloud the words and make an effort to sound out the italicized consonants clearly.

   *b*uy, ru*b*, *c*ame, *c*ar, arc*t*ic, *d*ay, *g*ame, *l*ow, *m*ay, *m*ine, ra*m*, *n*ice, pear, soa*p*, *s*o, *t*ale, ma*t*, *t*ie, an*t*, ea*t*, *v*eil, *v*i*v*id, *v*ault

2. The italicized letters are often sounded carelessly. Practice saying them aloud. Say the *u* as in *yoo*.

| | | |
|---|---|---|
| circ*u*lar | partic*u*lar | form*u*la |
| ed*u*cation | reg*u*lar | pop*u*lation |

3. Say the long *o*.

| | | | |
|---|---|---|---|
| mead*ow* | shall*ow* | yell*ow* | pill*ow* |

4. Be careful to say the *t* in to and the *th* in them.

| | | |
|---|---|---|
| see *them* | ought *to* | going *to* |
| trying *to* | try *them* | call *the* |

5. Say the *ing*. Do not omit the sound of *g*.

| | | |
|---|---|---|
| do*ing* | say*ing* | mak*ing* |
| go*ing* | study*ing* | help*ing* |
| see*ing* | sew*ing* | leav*ing* |
| hav*ing* | | |

6. Say the *t* and the *d*.

| | |
|---|---|
| don'*t* you | woul*d* you |
| tol*d* you | di*d* you |

☞ **Check your work on page 61. Record your score on page 64.**

## Pronunciation

*Pronunciation is saying a word correctly.*

Articulation is speaking clearly. **Pronunciation** is saying a word correctly. Pronunciation requires that you know what sounds to say when you say a word aloud. If you mispronounce a difficult or unusual word, you are not likely to be criticized. If you mispronounce common words you should know, you make a bad impression or fail to get across your meaning. Good articulation and pronunciation will give you the qualities of a well-spoken person.

If you do not know how to say a word, look it up in a dictionary. Sometimes, when you look up a word, you will find there are two or more ways to pronounce it. The writers of dictionaries consider the first pronunciation the one used more often.

Frequently mispronounced groups of words are listed below. Practice saying these words.

Do not turn around the order of the italicized letters in each of the following words.

Ap*ro*n

Hund*re*d

P*ro*posal

Child*re*n

The vowels in these words are sometimes mispronounced.

Catch (kach). Do not say "kich."

Genuine (jen´-yoo-en). Do not say "jen´-u-in."

Get (get). Do not say "git."

Maybe (ma´be). Do not say "mebbe."

Just (just). Do not say "jest."

Wrestling (res´ling). Do not saying "ras´ling."

Be sure to say the italicized letter in each word:

Reco*g*nize

Congra*t*ulations

Lib*r*ary

Represen*t*ative

Say only the syllables that are a part of each word. Do not add a syllable.

Athlete (ath´let)

Drowned (dround)

Burglar (bur´gler)

Film (film)

Elm (elm)

Grown (gron)

## CHECKPOINT 3–4

**YOUR GOAL:**
Get 3 or more answers correct.

Look up each of the following words in a dictionary. Decide which one of the pronunciations is most frequently used by careful speakers in your section of the country. Write the word in the space provided the way you think it should be pronounced. The first one is completed as an example. Give yourself 1 point for each correct answer.

- roof      **ruf** _____

1. apricot    _____

2. pecan     _____

3. pianist    _____

4. cheek     _____

5. greasy    _____

☞ **Check your work on page 61. Record your score on page 64.**

# ADDING QUALITY TO YOUR MESSAGE

After practicing and checking with others to see how you sound, you can think about adding even more quality to what you say by checking your posture, personal appearance, facial expression, and gestures.

## Posture

Your posture is important whether you are sitting down or standing up. If you are speaking and want others to pay attention to what you have to say, check your posture. Sit up straight and lean slightly forward as you speak.

If you are standing, stand up straight and distance yourself about 18 inches from the person(s) you are talking to. You probably have found it hard to pay attention to someone who is slouching on a couch or standing with drooping shoulders, or leaning against a wall. This kind of posture does not command attention and respect. The mechanic in Illustration 7-2 is demonstrating both poor and good speaking posture.

Illustration 3-2

Commanding respect with posture.

## MESSAGES FROM OTHERS

Tell me, I forget; show me, I remember; involve me, I understand.

—Chinese Proverb

### Personal Appearance

How you personally care for yourself sends a message about how you think of yourself. If you want others to hear you, you must give the appearance of self-confidence. Your clothes, your hairstyle, and personal grooming are seen by others as clues to your own self-image. Your personal appearance sends messages about not only how you feel about yourself but also how you relate to others. The old quote from Benjamin Disraeli, "Dress does not make a man, but it often makes a successful one," says it all.

### Facial Expression

Your face is very important in sending a message. Usually you read the face of someone who speaks to you. In fact, when you hear the words but cannot see the speaker's face, you may miss the real message being sent. Use your face. If you are sending a happy message, smile. If you are sending a sad message, look unhappy or sad. Help your listener by using your facial expression to help send a message. One study shows a person listening to you gets 7 percent of what you are saying from your words, 38 percent from your voice, and 55 percent from your facial expression. The study results indicate how important facial expression can be.

### Gestures

Your hands are very important when used to help send a message. They can emphasize a point, show a size or space (the bear's teeth were this big), show an action (she was wobbly on her feet), or demonstrate something by drawing it in the air. Use your hands to bring meaning to your words.

## CHECKPOINT 3–5

**YOUR GOAL:**
Get 3 or more answers correct.

Place a T in the space provided before the true statements. Place an F in the space provided before the false statements. The first one is completed as an example. Give yourself 1 point for each correct answer.

____F____ • Your posture is only important when you are standing and speaking.

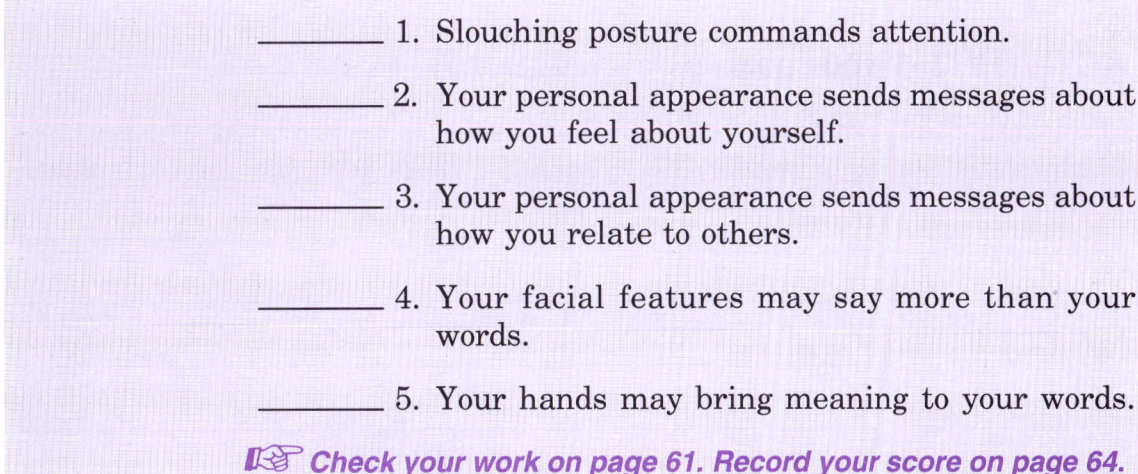

_____ 1. Slouching posture commands attention.

_____ 2. Your personal appearance sends messages about how you feel about yourself.

_____ 3. Your personal appearance sends messages about how you relate to others.

_____ 4. Your facial features may say more than your words.

_____ 5. Your hands may bring meaning to your words.

☞ *Check your work on page 61. Record your score on page 64.*

## WHAT YOU HAVE LEARNED

- The body parts which enable you to speak are: the brain, the nervous system, the vocal cords, and the mouth. They work automatically to give you the product of speech.
- The qualities of pitch, volume, tone, and inflection are necessary if your voice is going to be able to deliver an effective, clear message.
- The importance of correct articulation and pronunciation of words will enable you to be considered well spoken.
- In addition to speaking clearly, it is necessary that your posture, personal appearance, facial expression, and gestures help your voice deliver a message.

## ACTIVITY 3–1 YOUR GOAL: Get 2 or more answers correct.

Unscramble the important voice qualities in the space provided. The first one is completed as an example. Give yourself 1 point for each correct answer.

- note _____tone_____

1. hcipt _____

2. meovlu _____

3. niniolftce _____

☞ **Check your work on page 61. Record your score on page 64.**

## ACTIVITY 3–2 YOUR GOAL: Get 6 or more answers correct.

Place a T in the space provided if the statement is true. Place an F in the space provided if the statement is false. The first one is completed as an example. Give yourself 1 point for each correct answer.

_____T_____ • Tone is the quality of harshness or smoothness of a sound.

_____ 1. Most sounds in English should be made through the nose.

_____ 2. Inflection is the rising and falling of your voice.

_____ 3. A monotone voice is enjoyable to listen to.

_____ 4. The organ of articulation is the tongue.

_____ 5. Pronunciation is saying a word correctly.

_____ 6. The dictionary shows one way to pronounce each word correctly.

_____ 7. Listening to a very loud voice can be annoying.

_____ 8. There is no one right way to speak.

_____ 9. Pitch is the highness or lowness of a voice.

_____ 10. You have no control over the tension of your vocal cords, which determines the pitch of your voice.

☞ **Check your work on page 61. Record your score on page 64.**

**ACTIVITY 3–3** YOUR GOAL: Get 3 or more answers correct.

Look up each of the following words in a dictionary. Decide which one of the given pronunciations is most frequently used in your section of the country. Write the word the way you think it should be pronounced in the space provided. The first one is completed for you. Give yourself 1 point for each correct answer.

- Potato        pe-tat-o
- 1. Juvenile    _____
- 2. Iodine      _____
- 3. Forehead    _____
- 4  Tomato      _____
- 5. Aunt        _____

☞ **Check your work on page 61. Record your score on page 64.**

**ACTIVITY 3–4** YOUR GOAL: Get 3 or more answers correct.

In the space provided, unscramble the statements about adding quality to your spoken message. The first one is completed as an example. Give yourself 1 point for each correct answer.

- gnidnatS stureop si miropttan.

  **Standing posture is important.**
  _____

1. itS dna nael wardfor sa uoy kaeps.

   _____

2. ooPr erutsop seod ton mmcoand tttaennoi.

   _____

3. alnoserP ppaaeranec ssdne sssmeage.

   _____

4. wSho catnoi thiw ssureteg.

   _____

5. Faacli ssexprieon si miropttna.

   _____

☞ **Check your work on page 61. Record your score on page 64.**

# UNIT 4

## Your Chance to Speak Out

### WHAT YOU WILL LEARN

When you finish this unit you will be able to:

- Define and identify the purposes of a speech.
- Develop a speech from an outline.

## GIVING A SPEECH

Someday you may have the opportunity to speak to a group of people. You will want to take advantage of this opportunity. Speaking to a group may sound scary. However, if you are well prepared and have something to say, don't allow fear to cause you to turn down the opportunity to share your thoughts with others.

### What Is a Speech?

A speech is an occasion when a speaker delivers a message to cause some change in the people who are listening.

There are many possible reasons for giving a speech. A **speech** is defined as an occasion when a speaker delivers a message to cause some change in the people who are listening.

### Purposes of a Speech

Each speech has a purpose. Some key purposes follow in Illustration 4-1.

Illustration 4-1

Purposes of a speech.

### PURPOSES OF A SPEECH

A speech may be given to:

1. Give information to others.
2. Persuade others to do something.
3. Entertain others.
4. Inspire others.

40

## MESSAGES FROM OTHERS

The tones of human voices are mightier than strings of brass to move the human soul.

—Kropstock

It is good to rub and polish our brain against that of others.

—Montaigne

Give some thought to why you might someday want to give a speech. Do you believe drugs are harmful to young people? Chances are you do. Therefore, wouldn't you like to share your thoughts with young people attending a community meeting. A speech about the harmfulness of drugs would be presented to give information to others. Do you know a lot about a new method used in planting a crop? If so, you could give a speech to inspire others to give the method a try. Do you feel strongly about electing a certain candidate for city or county government? If you do, you could prepare a speech to persuade others to vote for your candidate. Do you know a funny story that would bring joy and laughter to others? You could tell this story in a speech to simply entertain a group of your friends.

## CHECKPOINT 4–1

**YOUR GOAL:**
List 2 or more topics.

In the space provided, list an example topic for each of the purposes for giving a speech. The first one is completed as an example. Give yourself 1 point for each example written.

**Purposes for Speeches**                          **Topic**

● Give information to others.  ● _How to Prepare a Special Meal._

1. Persuade others.          1. _____

_____

2. Entertain others.         2. _____

_____

3. Inspire others.           3. _____

_____

☞ *Check your work on page 61. Record your score on page 64.*

# DEVELOPING A SPEECH

In developing a speech, you will follow three steps. These steps are: selecting the subject, preparing the speech, and delivering the speech.

## Selecting the Subject

Sometimes the subject has been selected for you. Or, you have selected the subject based on your own purpose for giving the speech. However, you need to review three rules of selecting the subject to help tailor your subject to the audience and prepare the speech.

**Consider the Interests and Needs of the Audience First.** The purpose of any speech is to provide information so that the lives of the listeners will change and improve because of what you have shared. Direct your comments, examples, and stories to the audience. Be sure your audience can understand what you are talking about. For example, a speech at a union meeting on who to elect for union steward should include workplace examples and stories directed toward the interest of the audience. Each speech should make the listener feel that you are really talking to him or her. No speech should be given without relating what is being said to the listening audience.

**Consider What You Know about the Subject.** As you prepare to give a speech, jot down what you know about the subject. There may be areas you are not sure about. You may want to check your facts. You should think about what your audience wants to know. You will want to provide them with new information. Allow yourself time to make a visit to the library, talk to others, and check out facts and information as you prepare to give your speech.

Don't allow yourself to think thoughts like, "Gosh, no one will be interested in what I have to say. I'll just bore them." If you examine the interests and needs of your audience, organize your information, and present it with enthusiasm, your audience will be interested and will learn something from you.

**Do Not Make Your Topic Too Broad.** You want to be able to cover the topic in the time you have been given. For example, the topics "Food," "Automobiles," or "Gardening" are too broad. Break the topic into a manageable piece. "My Favorite Chinese Food," "The Car I Drive," or "How to Grow Petunias" would be topics to present in a short period of time. Remember the mind can only absorb what the seat can endure.

Illustration 4-2

Researching
your subject.

✔ **CHECKPOINT 4–2**

**YOUR GOAL:**
Get 2 or more
answers correct.

In the space provided, list the three rules of selecting the subject presented in this unit. Give yourself 1 point for each correct answer.

1. _____

_____

2. _____

_____

3. _____

_____

☞ *Check your work on page 61. Record your score on page 64.*

## Preparing the Speech

The preparation of the speech may be tough. Keep in mind that good preparation means success. Follow the steps of preparation with care.

1. Decide the specific purpose of your speech. Review the general purposes listed in Illustration 4-1. If you decide what it is you wish to tell the listener and why you wish to tell them, the rest of the organizing will be easier.

2. Use an outline to organize your speech. The speech outline has three major parts: introduction, body, and conclusion.

**Introduction.** You will first want to get the attention of your audience. There are many ways to do this: use an example, tell a story, use a shocking statement, or use a series of interesting facts.

**Body.** The body is simply telling the audience what it is you want them to know. The best way to tell the audience what you want them to know is to organize your information into logical points.

**Conclusion.** At the end of the speech, you will give a brief review of what has been said and tell the audience how what you have said will impact on them. The conclusion will be your last chance at getting your message across. There are several plans you may want to consider. You might use a personal example that shows the audience how valuable your information has been to them. You could tell a joke which shows the value of the information. You might repeat a portion of your opening sentence, to give your listener the feeling of having heard a complete speech. Or you could use a bold statement that shows the audience what will happen if it does not use the information given.

Now all you need to do is fill in the points you want to make within the outline. For example, suppose you have been asked by your community group to talk about "Living in a Large Family." Your outline might look something like this:

### LIVING IN A LARGE FAMILY

I.  Introduction—Short story about how mealtime can be a circus.

II. Body

    A. Attention from brothers and sisters

    B. Sharing attention from parents

    C. Space planning

    D. Sharing chores

III. Conclusion—Review the positive points and joys of a large family. Encourage others to see how the joy of a large family outweighs the worries about money, space, and other hardships.

The best way to write your outline notes is on index cards, as shown in Illustration 4-3. The cards can be easily held in your hand. You will want to write out and memorize the first and

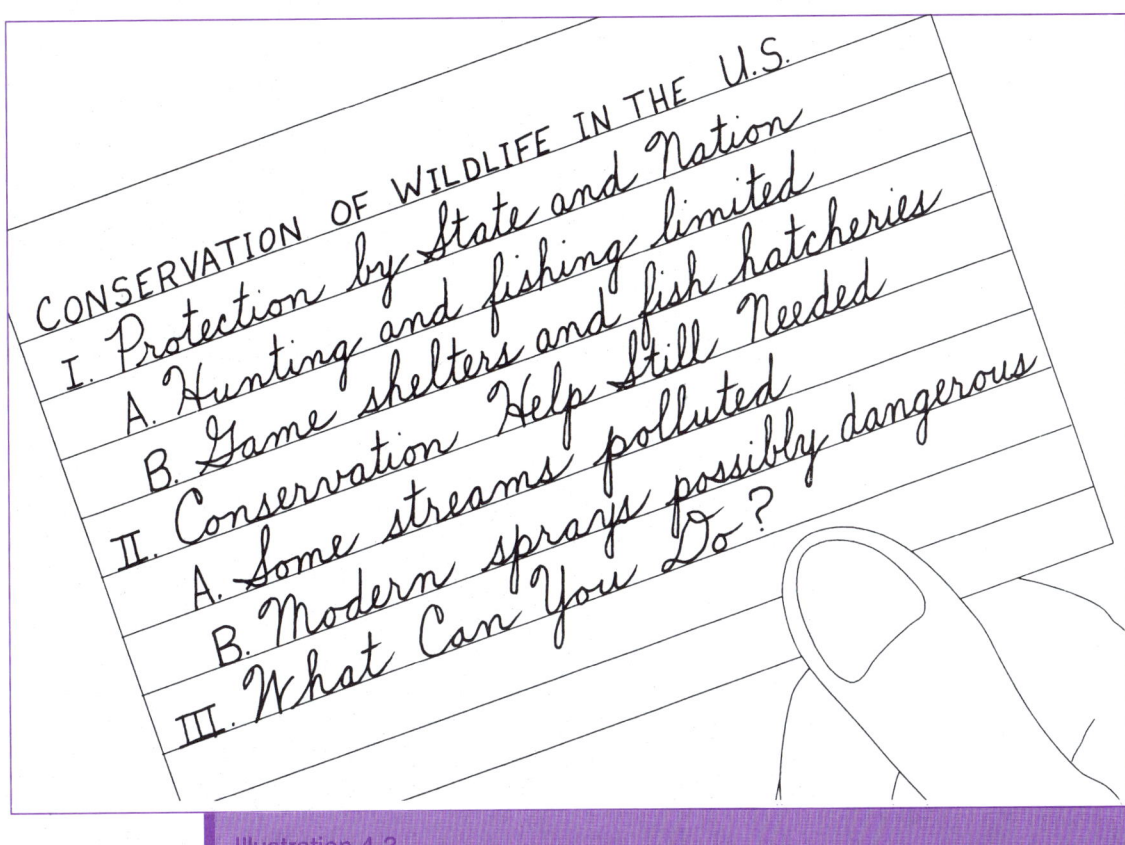

CONSERVATION OF WILDLIFE IN THE U.S.
I. Protection by State and Nation
   A. Hunting and fishing limited
   B. Game shelters and fish hatcheries
II. Conservation Help Still Needed
   A. Some streams polluted
   B. Modern sprays possibly dangerous
III. What Can You Do?

Illustration 4-3

Speech outline.

last sentence of your talk. You should choose the exact wording
of the rest of the talk while you are speaking. Then you won't
need to keep your eyes glued to your notes, and your talk will
sound lively. Of course, you will have spent some planning time
carefully thinking through what it is you want to present.

## CHECKPOINT 4–3

**YOUR GOAL:**
Write an
introduction.

Review the outline in Illustration 4-3. Write an introduction
for that speech in the space provided. Give yourself 1 point for
writing an introduction.

_____

_____

_____

_____

_____

☞ **Check your work on page 61. Record your score on page 64.**

## Delivering the Speech

Certainly the key to making a good speech is to have something interesting to say and to say it well and naturally. If you are nervous, practice your talk aloud at home. You may want to practice before a mirror. Give your speech to members of your family or friends. Then, when you are giving the speech before a larger group, imagine that you are talking to a friend.

When your opportunity to speak comes, walk quickly, forcefully, and confidently to the front of the room and wait quietly for everyone's attention before you begin. Look at the audience, smile, take a deep breath, and then begin to share your thoughts and ideas.

As you present your speech, keep in mind that you must be heard. You will need a pleasant voice with volume. If you speak to the people in the back of the room, your voice will be heard. You will loose your audience in a hurry if they cannot hear what you are saying.

Sometimes, as you are talking, you may find yourself stuck for a word or thought. If this happens, glance down at your notecards, think about what you have just said, and just wait until the word or thought comes. Do not fill in the time with "uh, uh . . ." Do not apologize to the audience if you get stuck. Just go on with the speech. Don't allow your body to detract from what you are saying.

Illustration 4-4

Practicing a speech.

Avoid meaningless and repeated gestures like scratching your head or pulling on your ear. Don't lean against a speaking podium or wall. Stand on both feet and don't rock from foot to foot. Examples of these distracting motions are shown in Illustration 4-5.

Illustration 4-5

These body motions will be speaking so loudly your audience will not be able to hear.

LEANING LENNIE

ITCHY IZZY

PULLING PAUL

ROCKING ROBERT

## MESSAGES FROM OTHERS

If you can't write your idea on the back of my calling card, you don't have a clear idea.

—David Belasco

Speak kind words, and you will hear kind echoes.

—Anonymous

Look mainly at your listeners. Glance only as you need to at your notes. Pick out four or five people in different parts of the room and speak to them, shifting your eyes from one to another.

Your speech may be supported by an exhibit, picture, or some other illustration. You may want to sketch or write some things on a chalkboard. If you choose, to support your words with these types of aids, don't forget you are talking to the audience. If an aid overwhelms the speech or draws constant attention to itself, it's not a good aid and should not be used.

As you approach the end of the speech, don't drift away with declining volume or lack of force. Give them your last line with force. Smile. Sit down. Don't end with, "I guess that's it," or "That's all I have to say," or "I can't think of anything else."

## CHECKPOINT 4–4

**YOUR GOAL:**
Get 4 or more answers correct.

Place a T in the space provided if the statement is true. Place an F in the space provided if the statement is false. The first one is completed as an example. Give yourself 1 point for each correct answer.

_____**F**_____ • A good line to end a speech would be "That's all I have to say."

_____ 1. Practice is not necessary if you have given adequate thought to preparing a speech.

_____ 2. Wait for everyone's attention before beginning a speech.

_____ 3. Adjust the volume of your voice so that you are talking to the audience in the front row.

_____ 4. You should apologize to the audience if you get stuck for a word or thought.

_____ 5. Avoid scratching your head or making other meaningless gestures as you speak.

_____ 6. Avoid looking at your audience.

_____ 7. A smile at the beginning and ending of a speech is appropriate.

☞ **Check your work on page 61. Record your score on page 64.**

## WHAT YOU HAVE LEARNED

- The purpose of a speech may be to give information to others, persuade others, entertain others, or to inspire others.
- A good speech is constructed by preparing an outline which will include an introduction to get the attention of the audience, a body of information you want to share with the audience, and a conclusion, which will review what the audience has been told and how the information will impact them.

## ACTIVITY 4–1 YOUR GOAL: Get 2 or more answers correct.

In the space provided, give the purpose of the speech topic described in the left column. The first one is completed as an example. Give yourself 1 point for each correct answer.

| Topic | Purpose of Speech |
|---|---|
| • How to Make Bread | Give information to others |
| 1. Vote for Joe Smith for City Council | _____ |
| 2. A Summer Vacation to Remember | _____ |
| 3. Feel Better About Yourself | _____ |

☞ **Check your work on page 61. Record your score on page 64.**

## ACTIVITY 4–2 YOUR GOAL: Get 3 or more answers correct.

Place a T in the space provided if the statement is true. Place an F in the space provided if the statement is false. The first one is completed as an example. Give yourself 1 point for each correct answer.

____F____ • All speeches are written to entertain.

_____ 1. Check your facts before presenting them.

_____ 2. No topic is too broad for a speech.

_____ 3. You will always get to select the subject for your speech.

_____ 4. You should consider the interests and needs of the audience you are speaking to.

_____ 5. The purpose of any speech is to provide information that will change and improve the lives of the audience.

☞ **Check your work on page 61. Record your score on page 64.**

## ACTIVITY 4–3 YOUR GOAL: Get 2 or more answers correct.

In the space provided, list the purpose of the three parts of the speech.

Introduction: _____

_____

_____

Body: _____

_____

_____

_____

Conclusion: _____

_____

_____

_____

☞ **Check your work on page 62. Record your score on page 64.**

## ACTIVITY 4–4 YOUR GOAL: Get 3 or more answers correct.

Place an X in the space provided if the statement is a good speaking habit.
Place an O in the space provided if the statement is a poor speaking habit.
The first one is completed as an example. Give yourself 1 point for each correct answer.

___O___ ● Rocking back and forth while speaking.

_____ 1. Using notecards.

_____ 2. Taking a deep breath before beginning a speech.

_____ 3. Talking to the people in the back row.

_____ 4. Leaning against the podium.

_____ 5. Looking at the audience.

☞ **Check your work on page 62. Record your score on page 64.**

# CHECKING WHAT YOU LEARNED

Now you can see how much you have learned about speaking. These 25 questions cover the main topics you studied in this book. There is not a time limit, so take your time.

When you finish, check your answers. Give yourself 2 points for each correct answer. Record your score on your Personal Progress Record. The evaluation chart will tell you where you may need additional study.

DIRECTIONS:    Read each of the following statements. If the statement is true, write a T in the space provided. If it is false, write an F in the space provided.

_____  1.   Listening to the sound of an engine motor is communicating.
_____  2.   The only purpose of messages is to give information or direction.
_____  3.   A message sent with words is a verbal message.
_____  4.   The actions of the receiver of a message are called connectors.
_____  5.   The circle of communication is complete when the sender's message reaches the receiver.
_____  6.   A loud booming voice is needed in the workplace.
_____  7.   A major part of speaking on the job will be sharing and providing information to others.
_____  8.   Avoid referring questions to others.
_____  9.   Persuasion is an attempt to get others to agree with you.
_____ 10.   Ask questions in the employment job interview.
_____ 11.   What you say at the employment interview may determine whether or not you get the job.
_____ 12.   Your vocal cords vibrate to create the vocal sounds.
_____ 13.   Each person's voice is the same.
_____ 14.   Your brain, nervous system, vocal cords, and throat work to make you hear.
_____ 15.   Volume is the loudness or softness of your voice.
_____ 16.   A monotone voice has good expression.
_____ 17.   Good posture commands respect.
_____ 18.   Your facial features may say more than your words.
_____ 19.   The purpose of the introduction of a speech is to tell the audience what you want them to know.
_____ 20.   Practicing a speech will make the speech sound unnatural.
_____ 21.   Avoid meaningless and repeated gestures when you are giving a speech.
_____ 22.   Apologize to the audience if you get stuck for a word or thought while speaking.
_____ 23.   One way to conclude a speech is to tell a joke.

_____ 24.  In developing a speech, consider your interests and needs first.

_____ 25.  Lean against the podium or a wall for support as you present a speech.

☞ *Check your work on page 62. Record your score on page 65.*

# GLOSSARY

## A

**Articulate.** To make sounds more clearly. Also called enunciation.

## C

**Channel.** The route which a message takes to get to the receiver.

**Communication.** The process of sending and receiving information.

## F

**Feedback.** The actions of the receiver of a message.

## I

**Inflection.** The rising and falling of your voice.

## M

**Message.** The item of communication that is sent or received.

**Monotone.** A voice with no expression. It always sounds the same.

## N

**Nonverbal message.** A message sent without using words.

## P

**Persuasion.** The attempt to get others to adopt or agree with an idea that you have.

**Pitch.** The highness or lowness of a voice.

**Pronunciation.** Saying a word correctly.

## S

**Speech.** An occasion when a speaker delivers a message to cause some change in the people who are listening.

## T

**Tone.** The quality of harshness or smoothness of a sound.

## V

**Verbal message.** A message sent using words.

**Volume.** The loudness or softness of a voice.

# ▲▲▲ INDEX

# ANSWERS

✔ **CHECKING WHAT YOU KNOW**

| | |
|---|---|
| 1. T | 14. T |
| 2. F | 15. F |
| 3. T | 16. F |
| 4. T | 17. T |
| 5. F | 18. T |
| 6. F | 19. F |
| 7. T | 20. F |
| 8. F | 21. T |
| 9. F | 22. F |
| 10. F | 23. F |
| 11. T | 24. T |
| 12. T | 25. F |
| 13. T | |

## UNIT 1

### CHECKPOINT 1–1, page 3

Sample answers:

List two messages or sounds most often heard in the city.

1. Traffic noises.
2. Roar of a truck.

List two messages or sounds received from someone today.

1. The message to call a friend.
2. Directions to a doctor's office.

List two messages or sounds you like to receive in the country.

1. The soft "moo" of a cow.
2. The chirp of a robin.

### CHECKPOINT 1–2, page 4

Sample answers:

List four messages which give information that you have sent today.

1. Told your child to go to school.
2. Offered to work overtime.
3. Told a friend how to find the Social Services office.
4. Told a neighbor the bus fare to downtown.

List four warnings you have given today or in the past.

1. Don't go into the water for two hours after eating.
2. Watch out for the person on the motorcycle!
3. The dog bites!
4. Stay inside the safety lines.

Write out a direction you have given or plan to give today.

1. Send the rent check to the landlord. The address is 1415 Winter Street, Lincoln, NE 68506-1415. The checkbook is in the top drawer in the kitchen cabinet next to the sink. A stamp and envelope are on top of the refrigerator.
2. Joel lives on Spring Street. Stay on the north side of the street and walk down to the first light. Turn to your right and walk one block to Spring Street. Joel's house is white with green trim and has a chain-link fence.

### CHECKPOINT 1–3, page 6

Your answers may vary. Nonverbal messages do not mean the same thing to everyone.

1. Tense or a nervous person. Perhaps annoyed about something.
2. Excited about something. Mad about something and showing anger.
3. Tense. Anticipating something that is about to happen.
4. Defensive mood. Unhappy about something. Not open to suggestion.
5. Giving sharp, accusing directions.

### CHECKPOINT 1–4, page 9

| | Sight | Sound | Touch |
|---|---|---|---|
| 1. | | | X |
| 2. | | | X |
| 3. | | X | |

### ACTIVITY 1–1, page 10

There are no specific answers in the activity. Did you review the cartoon to find a sender and a listener? Did you notice that many cartoons are funny because the circle of communication is not complete?

### ACTIVITY 1–2, page 10

There are no specific answers. A sample of

five is listed.
1. Shaking a fist
2. Pulling on an ear
3. Rubbing the nose
4. Frowning
5. Winking

## ACTIVITY 1–3, page 11

Your answers may vary. Compare your answers with someone else after the activity is complete.

1. The man has been skiing and broke his leg.
2. The woman is poor and homeless.
3. The student is tired or uninterested.
4. It is the Fourth of July.
5. A loved one is ill or has died.

## UNIT 2

## CHECKPOINT 2–1, page 14

1. be
2. provide /give
3. saying
4. control
5. clearly

## CHECKPOINT 2–2, page 16

1. F
2. T
3. T
4. T
5. T
6. F
7. T
8. T

## CHECKPOINT 2–3, page 19

1. questions
2. requests
3. explain
4. attempt
5. story

## CHECKPOINT 2–4, page 21

There are no specific answers to this exercise. Some possible answers are given below:

1. I have been a stock clerk in the produce department for a large grocery store.
2. I enjoy working outdoors very much. This is one of the reasons I am seeking employment with the forestry service.
3. I could begin working for the forestry service after giving a two-week notice to my present employer.
4. I would be successful because I love the outdoors and I am concerned about the future of our environment.
5. I would be willing to travel if the position requires it.

## CHECKPOINT 2–5, page 23

1. Listen carefully.
2. Ask questions to clarify the concerns.
3. State your side of the story.
4. Indicate that you will work to improve.
5. Thank the reviewer for his or her time.

## ACTIVITY 2–1, page 25

1. X  You were willing to help Meredith. You were looking for more information to help her.
2. O  You did not ask if Ileana understood the directions.
3. O  Your answer was appropriate, but you used the opportunity to begin a nonwork-related conversation.

## ACTIVITY 2–2, page 26

There are no specific answers to this exercise. Here are some sample answers:
1. Did you know this ice cream is low in calories?
2. Do you remember the hours I filled in for you so that you could attend your son's graduation?
3. I didn't like the new idea either until Joe showed me how much time I could save.
4. Do you know that Slide Soap is used in the White House?

## ACTIVITY 2–3, page 27

There are no specific answers to this exercise. Some possible answers are given below:
1. Why do you want to work here?
2. I would like to work here because of the pleasant working conditions and fair wages.
3. How can I improve my work?

Answers

## UNIT 3

### CHECKPOINT 3–1, page 29

1. T
2. T
3. F
4. T
5. T

### CHECKPOINT 3–2, page 31

There is no specific key to this exercise. Read each group of sentences to someone twice.

### CHECKPOINT 3–3, page 32

Read each group of words to someone else.

### CHECKPOINT 3–4, page 34

1. ap´-re-kät
2. pi´-kän
3. pe-an´-est
4. chek
5. gre-se

### CHECKPOINT 3–5, page 36

1. F
2. T
3. T
4. T
5. T

### ACTIVITY 3–1, page 38

1. pitch
2. volume
3. inflection

### ACTIVITY 3–2, page 38

| | |
|---|---|
| 1. F | 6. F |
| 2. T | 7. T |
| 3. F | 8. T |
| 4. T | 9. T |
| 5. T | 10. F |

### ACTIVITY 3–3, page 39

1. jü´-ve-nil
2. i´-e-din
3. for´-ed
4. te-mat´-o
5. ant

### Activity 3–4, page 39

1. Sit and lean forward as you speak.
2. Poor posture does not command attention.
3. Personal appearance sends messages.
4. Show action with gestures.
5. Facial expression is important.

## UNIT 4

### CHECKPOINT 4–1, page 41

There are no specific answers for this exercise. Sample answers are given below:
1. Vote for Olivia Zapata
2. My Dog Can't Do Tricks
3. Give Yourself a Break

### CHECKPOINT 4–2, page 43

1. Consider what you know about the subject.
2. Consider the interests and needs of the audience first.
3. Do not make your topic too broad.

### CHECKPOINT 4–3, page 45

There are no specific answers for this exercise. Sample answer is given below:
The nation's wildlife population is in danger. Do you care enough to do something about it!

### CHECKPOINT 4–4, page 48

1. F
2. T
3. F
4. F
5. T
6. F
7. T

### ACTIVITY 4–1, page 50

1. persuade
2. entertain
3. inspire

### ACTIVITY 4–2, page 50

1. T
2. F
3. F
4. T
5. T

## ACTIVITY 4–3, page 50

Introduction: Part of a speech that is written to get the attention of the audience.

Body: The information you want the audience to know.

Conclusion: Brief review of the speech and the impact it will have on the audience.

## ACTIVITY 4–4, page 51

1. X
2. X
3. X
4. O
5. X

## ✔ CHECKING WHAT YOU LEARNED

| | |
|---|---|
| 1. T | 14. F |
| 2. F | 15. T |
| 3. T | 16. F |
| 4. F | 17. T |
| 5. F | 18. T |
| 6. F | 19. F |
| 7. T | 20. F |
| 8. F | 21. T |
| 9. T | 22. F |
| 10. T | 23. T |
| 11. T | 24. F |
| 12. T | 25. F |
| 13. F | |

# PERSONAL PROGRESS RECORD

Name: _____

## ✔ CHECKING WHAT YOU KNOW

Use the chart below to determine the areas you need to do the most work. In the space provided, write the total number of points you got right for each content area. Then add up the total number of points right to find your final score. Circle those items you answered correctly. As you begin your study, pay close attention to those areas where you missed half or more of the questions.

| Content Area | Item Numbers | Study Pages | Total Points | Number Right |
|---|---|---|---|---|
| **UNIT 1** | | | | |
| Communicating | 1, 2, 3 | 1-5 | 6 | |
| Circle of Communication | 4, 5 | 6-8 | 4 | |
| **UNIT 2** | | | | |
| Preparing for Being a Speaker | 6, 7 | 12-14 | 4 | |
| Speaking Situations on the Job | 8, 9 | 15-19 | 4 | |
| Special Opportunities on the Job for Speaking | 10, 11 | 20-24 | 4 | |
| **UNIT 3** | | | | |
| What It Takes to Speak | 12, 13, 14 | 28-29 | 6 | |
| Improving Your Speaking | 15, 16 | 30-31 | 4 | |
| Adding Quality to Your Message | 17, 18 | 35-36 | 4 | |
| **UNIT 4** | | | | |
| Developing a Speech | 19, 20, 21, 22 23, 24, 25 | 42-48 | 14 | |

Date _____    Total Points: 50    Your Score: [     ]

## UNIT 1: Communicating with Others

| Exercise | Score |
|---|---|
| Checkpoint 1-1 | _____ |
| Checkpoint 1-2 | _____ |
| Checkpoint 1-3 | _____ |
| Checkpoint 1-4 | _____ |
| Activity 1-1 | _____ |
| Activity 1-2 | _____ |
| Activity 1-3 | _____ |
| TOTAL | _____ |

**HOW ARE YOU DOING?**

| | |
|---|---|
| 29 or better | Excellent |
| 24-28 | Good |
| 19-23 | Fair |
| Less than 19 | See Instructor |

## UNIT 2: Speaking in the Workplace

| Exercise | Score |
|---|---|
| Checkpoint 2-1 | _____ |
| Checkpoint 2-2 | _____ |
| Checkpoint 2-3 | _____ |
| Checkpoint 2-4 | _____ |
| Checkpoint 2-5 | _____ |
| Activity 2-1 | _____ |
| Activity 2-2 | _____ |
| Activity 2-3 | _____ |
| TOTAL | _____ |

**HOW ARE YOU DOING?**

| | |
|---|---|
| 22 or better | Excellent |
| 17-21 | Good |
| 12-16 | Fair |
| Less than 12 | See Instructor |

## UNIT 3: Polishing Your Speaking Skills

| Exercise | Score |
|---|---|
| Checkpoint 3-1 | _____ |
| Checkpoint 3-2 | _____ |
| Checkpoint 3-3 | _____ |
| Checkpoint 3-4 | _____ |
| Checkpoint 3-5 | _____ |
| Activity 3-1 | _____ |
| Activity 3-2 | _____ |
| Activity 3-3 | _____ |
| Activity 3-4 | _____ |
| TOTAL | _____ |

**HOW ARE YOU DOING?**

| | |
|---|---|
| 29 or better | Excellent |
| 24-28 | Good |
| 19-23 | Fair |
| Less than 19 | See Instructor |

## UNIT 4: Your Chance to Speak Out

| Exercise | Score |
|---|---|
| Checkpoint 4-1 | _____ |
| Checkpoint 4-2 | _____ |
| Checkpoint 4-3 | _____ |
| Checkpoint 4-4 | _____ |
| Activity 4-1 | _____ |
| Activity 4-2 | _____ |
| Activity 4-3 | _____ |
| Activity 4-4 | _____ |
| TOTAL | _____ |

**HOW ARE YOU DOING?**

| | |
|---|---|
| 19 or better | Excellent |
| 14-18 | Good |
| 9-13 | Fair |
| Less than 9 | See Instructor |

Name: _____

Use the chart below to determine the areas you need to do the most review. In the space provided, write the total number of points you got right for each content area. Review those areas where you missed half or more of the questions. Then add up the total number of points right to find your final score.

| Content Area | Item Numbers | Study Pages | Total Points | Number Right |
|---|---|---|---|---|
| **UNIT 1** | | | | |
| Communicating | 1, 2, 3 | 1-5 | 6 | |
| Circle of Communication | 4, 5 | 6-8 | 4 | |
| **UNIT 2** | | | | |
| Preparing for Being a Speaker | 6, 7 | 12-14 | 4 | |
| Speaking Situations on the Job | 8, 9 | 15-19 | 4 | |
| Special Opportunities on the Job for Speaking | 10, 11 | 20-24 | 4 | |
| **UNIT 3** | | | | |
| What It Takes to Speak | 12, 13, 14 | 28-29 | 6 | |
| Improving Your Speaking | 15, 16 | 30-31 | 4 | |
| Adding Quality to Your Message | 17, 18 | 35-36 | 4 | |
| **UNIT 4** | | | | |
| Developing a Speech | 19, 20, 21, 22 23, 24, 25 | 42-48 | 14 | |

Date _____     Total Points: 50     Your Score: [____]